My Neighborhood
The Fire Station

Aaron Carr

www.av2books.com

LET'S READ
AV²
BY WEIGL™
ADDED VALUE • AUDIO VISUAL

Go to **www.av2books.com,** and enter this book's unique code.

BOOK CODE

J248373

AV² by Weigl brings you media enhanced books that support active learning.

AV² provides enriched content that supplements and complements this book. Weigl's AV² books strive to create inspired learning and engage young minds in a total learning experience.

Your AV² Media Enhanced books come alive with...

Audio
Listen to sections of the book read aloud.

Video
Watch informative video clips.

Embedded Weblinks
Gain additional information for research.

Try This!
Complete activities and hands-on experiments.

Key Words
Study vocabulary, and complete a matching word activity.

Quizzes
Test your knowledge.

Slide Show
View images and captions, and prepare a presentation.

... and much, much more!

Published by AV² by Weigl
350 5th Avenue, 59th Floor New York, NY 10118
Website: www.av2books.com   www.weigl.com

Library of Congress Cataloging-in-Publication Data

Carr, Aaron.
 The fire station / Aaron Carr.
    p. cm. -- (My neighborhood)
 Audience: K to grade 3.
 ISBN 978-1-62127-344-8 (hardcover : alk. paper) -- ISBN 978-1-62127-349-3 (softcover : alk. paper)
 1. Fire stations--Juvenile literature. 2. Fire extinction--Juvenile literature. 3. Fire fighters--Juvenile literature. I. Title.
 TH9148.C336 2014
 628.9'25--dc23

                    2013006840

Printed in the United States of America in North Mankato, Minnesota
3 4 5 6 7 8 9 0 18 17 16 15 14

052014
WEP010514

Project Coordinators: Heather Kissock and Megan Cuthbert Design: Mandy Christiansen

Weigl acknowledges Getty Images as the primary image supplier for this title.

The Fire Station

CONTENTS

This is my neighborhood.

The fire station is in my neighborhood.

People call the fire station when there is a fire.

6

They also call the fire station if they are in danger.

I see firefighters in my neighborhood.

Firefighters put out fires. They keep the people and buildings in my neighborhood safe.

Firefighters use fire trucks to help put out fires.

Fire trucks have hoses and ladders that reach high places.

TO REPORT A FIRE
DIAL 911

The fire station has a large garage. This is where the fire trucks are parked.

The garage also has tools for fighting fires.

Firefighters help people in my neighborhood who are hurt.

Sometimes they save people and animals.

Firefighters make sure the buildings in my neighborhood are safe.

They show people what tools to use to stop a fire.

I can visit the fire station with my class from school.

Sometimes I even get to use the firefighter's gear.

Firefighters take part in neighborhood events.

They ride in parades and teach people about fire safety.

See what you have learned about fire stations and firefighters.

22